Instruction Manual for Your Child

The One You Wish Your Child Came With

by

Michael Raskind, MSW, LCSW

authorHOUSE®

AuthorHouse™
1663 Liberty Drive, Suite 200
Bloomington, IN 47403
www.authorhouse.com
Phone: 1-800-839-8640

First published by AuthorHouse 6/29/2008

ISBN: 978-1-4343-8022-7 (sc)

Library of Congress Control Number: 2008903465

Printed in the United States of America
Bloomington, Indiana

This book is printed on acid-free paper.

Inspiration

The manual was inspired by two decades of work with parents who were looking for a simplified way to raise their family without having to read several books and pay for hours of parenting classes or therapy (when it is not necessary). Since every parent wishes that they had an owner's manual for their children; I felt that it should be written! Though there is tons of information that could have been included in the manual; the focus was to create a hands on, to the point resource.

Michael Raskind MSW

THE RELATIONSHIP

When one builds a house, engineers will tell you it's best to start with the foundation. Then the framing, then the floors and the walls come after. If a house is built without a proper foundation, it would not stay sound when storms or other natural disasters should come upon it.

The same is true for relationships. The foundation of a family is drawn upon two elements: The nature of the parent to parent relationship and the nature of the parent-child relationship. When these are strong and positive, then the rest of the home will be strong and positive. Let us look at what is necessary for these two relationships.

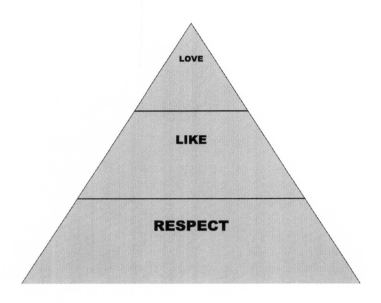

This pyramid represents what all family relationships should contain. All human relationships do not contain all three of these. Can you guess the common denominator?

Respect <u>must</u> exist in all human relationships. Even the worse of enemies have a modicum of respect for each other. They may not like each other, they may feel no love, but there is usually a mutual respect. Respect is the foundation and the biggest section of life's pyramid because we have more people in our lives that we don't necessarily like or love, but have respect for. These folks may include the mailman, teachers, police officers, clergy, coworkers, and bosses and a lot of people we have never met.

After this level, we have those in our lives that we both **respect and like**. These are people we actually know, and are somewhat close to. Certain teachers, our own clergy, acquaintances, club members…

We can respect someone and not like them, but we can not like someone without respecting them.

The last category is exclusive. It is the people we **love**. We must both have respect and like in order to love them. Too often in my practice have I heard couples say that they love their spouse but do not like or respect them. I want to make it very clear at this point it is **impossible** to love someone unless you like and respect the person. This is different from not respecting or liking what someone did. What someone does is not necessarily reflective of their character unless a pattern arises.

Imagine for a moment if respect were to erode from a relationship

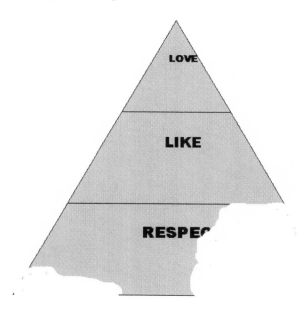

As a relationship loses respect the foundation becomes at risk and eventually will topple over. In order to keep things standing, people will take away some like and love, but what they're left with is not a pyramid, but a distortion leading to unhappiness for everyone. When families came to me for relationship therapy, they often wanted me to help them bring love back into their lives. Were I started was always to build respect.

If you want respect you'll have to earn it! This statement is infamous and the reason why so many relationships go bad. It is an absurd idea, that basic human respect must be earned! As parents, you must always maintain respect for your children, as we expect that they must respect their parents. When they behave disrespectful towards you, you must continue to model for them respect by treating them (and each other) with respect.

But, what is respect? We know what it is because we know how we feel when someone disrespects us. We feel, hurt, we feel invaded, we feel unloved. So what is it that is occurring that causes this?

Walls and fences have two (2) main purposes: To keep things in and other things out! Personal boundaries are very much the same. They are **semi permeable** in that we allow crossing of our boundaries only by certain people. An example of a semi permeable boundary is a coffee filter. When we make coffee we put the ground coffee in a filter and pour water on it. The water soaks through the coffee and goes through the filter, but the grounds are not allowed to pass and go through into the pot! We all know how distasteful it is when we get grounds in our coffee! Our personal boundaries work the same: While our spouse can hug and kiss us; it would be a breach of our boundaries if a stranger should do this to us.

The following diagram depicts what boundaries are. The **Self**, who we are, our very being, is at the center. Anything that crosses a boundary can change who the self is. The first boundary, the very outer most ring, is our **physical** boundary. This boundary includes our body, our food, and our belongings; whenever someone forces themself through this boundary they are being disrespectful. Examples are: Hitting, pinching, imprisoning, taking or touching our belongings, withholding food or medicine. Even hugging or kissing can be breaking a boundary.

The next boundary is **Social**. This is a tricky boundary, especially with our children. We must limit who our children are friends with because they do not know how to form positive social ties. However, as adults we often impinge upon our spouses that they can not be friends with someone simply because we do not like them! This is disrespectful and endangers the family.

The next boundary is the cognitive or **Thought** boundary. This is when we try to control another's thoughts or put down their ideas. One must avoid being the "Thought Police" when dealing with others. No one has the right to put down your thoughts; as you do not have the right to do this to others. Children can think whatever they like; thinking is a private matter. When they express thoughts that you don't understand, you may ask them to clarify and give examples or ask questions. Eventually, the children will develop their thoughts and beliefs. Never, make anyone feel stupid because you don't like their ideas.

Related to thought, is the **Emotional** boundary. This boundary is crossed in a disrespectful manner more than any other. How often we cross this boundary by saying or doing things that are hurtful.

The last boundary is **Spiritual**. This is not necessarily religion. Religion is only a small part of this boundary. What makes us feel alive, what we like to do in life is the spiritual. Some people love to go skiing; I don't. To keep someone from doing what they love in life is disrespectful because it damages the spirit.

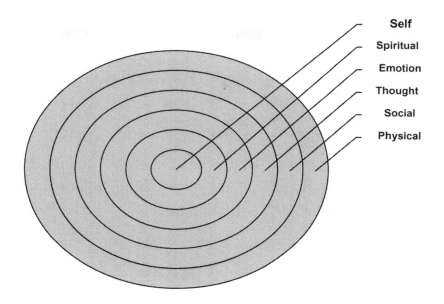

Anytime we cross a boundary without permission, we are being **disrespectful**. Helping someone to build and maintain healthy boundaries is called being **respectful**! One of the most disrespectful things a person can do to themselves is to misuse alcohol and to take drugs. Both drugs and alcohol affect our boundaries. They change us physically, socially, and emotionally. Our thinking can become distorted, and chronic abusers change the things in life they love.

Often parent's wonder if their children came with an owner's manual. After all, even your automobile comes with one and I have seen instructions for a flashlight! The most important job in the world and no instructions or manual comes with the baby!

When the kids are behaving, we are so proud of ourselves, and when they are not behaving, we cannot quite put a finger on what we are doing wrong! It is my intention in this booklet to outline simply and as directly as possible the science of behavior and how you can modify your child's behavior easily and with little if any cost!

It is important to understand that this booklet is not meant to replace needed family or individual counseling. It <u>may</u> not circumvent the need for medication(s). However, after 20 years as a child and family therapist, I can say that the following parenting methods have proven themselves effective time and time again as long as the parent or parents stick to them.

THE TRUTH ABOUT BEHAVIOR

Ask yourself; how many types of behavior are there? For your first exercise, I would like you to take a sheet of paper and list the types of behavior there are. This exercise should only take 5 minutes.

STOP!
DO NOT READ ON UNTIL YOU HAVE COMPLETED THIS EXERCISE.

BEHAVIORS:

Now that you have your list of behavior types, I would like you to break them down into three categories. These three categories represent how 90% of parents, I have worked with, group their children's behavior. They are *Good*, *Bad* and *Supposed To*. You should now have three columns: Column one labeled Good Behavior. Column two labeled Bad Behavior and Column three labeled Supposed To Behavior.

This is how most parents see behavior, either with their kids, neighbors, friends, and coworkers. **However, it is wrong!**

Reality is that there are only two types of behavior *NEGATIVE* and *POSITIVE*. There is no such thing as behavior that is "supposed to behavior!" If a child does what he or she is supposed to do it is positive! If he or she does not do what is supposed to be done then it is negative! The next exercise takes a lot of time and patience. It must be done when you and your child will both be at home.

EXERCISE: Take a large pad of paper and on the top write my child's behaviors. From the moment your child wakes up I want you to write down everything the child does from getting dressed, putting clothes in hamper (or not), opening bedroom door, closing the door, running, going to the bathroom, eating, picking their nose, playing… get the idea? This will take all-day, afternoon and night until they go to bed.

When you are done, come back to this booklet for further instructions.

STOP!

DO NOT READ ON UNTIL YOU HAVE COM-PLETED THIS EXERCISE.

CHILD'S NAME:

BEHAVIORS:

Now that you are completely exhausted and have gone through a ream of paper I want you to look at each item and mark a (+) or (–)sign next to each item. Every entry must have either a (+) or (–)sign. Do not leave any blank and *do not put two signs for the same entry*.

Now count how many +'s and how many –'s there are. Most people report over twice as many positives as negatives. What is your tally? Now, next to each item, whether it is a (+) or a (–) write down the symbol (*) for each item that you reacted to. For example, if you praised them put a (*) or if you reprimanded them, punished them etc put a (*). Now, let's study your findings. What most people see is that though there are more + behaviors than – behaviors, the – behaviors received much more attention from you than the + ones**! Why?** Because we still look at behaviors in three categories: good, bad and supposed to! We rarely praise supposed to behaviors, we only **sometimes** praise positive behaviors, and nearly always jump quickly on the negative! So as a child, if mommy or daddy gives me attention more often for the negatives and it is attention I crave, what behavior would most often be exhibited when I really want attention? Negative of course!

What Is Reinforcement?

Behavioral scientists talk about reinforcing behavior. There are three basic types of behavioral interventions: Positive Reinforcement, Negative Reinforcement, and Punishment. All three of these are effective for changing behavior. However, they work in varying degrees.

Punishment is the least effective. Even with animals we find that this is less likely to work, or takes longer to work than the other two. For example, if you put a dog in a cage and want him to stand in the right rear corner, you could electrify the bottom of the cage, (only to cause some discomfort) each time the dog stands in the wrong corner. Eventually, the dog will learn to stand in the right rear corner. We punish people for breaking rules by putting them in jail. The recidivism rate (rate of repeat offenders) shows that punishment does not work the best.

Negative reinforcement is the act of taking away an unpleasant stimulus or condition when a person behaves appropriately. In animals, using the same example as above, we would electrify the entire bottom of the cage and turn off the electricity only when the dog stands in the right rear corner. Eventually, the dog learns to stand in the right rear corner. With people we let them out of jail on "early release" when they behave well. These people have a slightly better chance of not ending up back in jail than those who complete their full jail term.

Positive reinforcement is the giving of a reward for positive or desirable behavior. In the dog example above, we can give the dog a snack each time it stands in the right rear corner (putting the snack in the right rear corner of the cage). This technique trains the dog the quickest and in the most humane way. People, who have a history of positive parenting, where they are rewarded for positive behavior, tend not to break the law and go to jail. Though we do know that this is not always true; it is more often the case than not.

Punishment Vs Discipline

One of the hardest concepts to overcome for many people is that discipline and punishment are not the same. Punishment is rarely done to teach a lesson, but more often out of retribution or anger from the parent. Many times punishments such as spankings, isolation (sending to a corner) are invoked because the parent feels hurt, jilted, vengeful, or powerless (and uses a physical approach to regain power).

Discipline is an art. We talk of the disciplines of painting, philosophy, teaching and so forth. When one disciplines, we put our anger aside and find ways to teach our children, to guide them along a better path. We help them to put discipline into their lives. The term "spare the rod, spoil the child" is often seen as a biblical consent for physical punishment or spanking. However, this verse does not even appear in any biblical writings! In biblical times a rod or staff was used to guide; for example Moses, Kings, and even a Shepherd used their staffs or rods to guide or as a symbol of leadership. We must also use our experience and know how (our staffs) to guide our children along life's path in a disciplined loving manner.

POWER OF
POSITIVE AFFIRMATIONS

Thinking in a positive way will beget positive results while thinking negatively will beget negative results. This message has been part of our belief system for thousands of years: For example, the Bible. Successful people have hammered this home in their books and tapes: <u>The Power of Positive Thinking,</u> by Norman Vincent Peale, <u>Success through a Positive Mental Attitude,</u> by W. Clement Stone, <u>How to Win Friends and Influence People</u> by Dale Carnegie. Writing down what we want and how we plan to achieve it and reading it over and over every day, several times a day, helps us to keep our goals alive and our activities in line with achieving them.

This is also true with parenting. Parents need to write down their goals and how they want to achieve them with their children. They need to make posters of positive statements that are constant reminders of what they are trying to achieve. They need to hang these in their homes, offices and automobiles. Only in this way will old ineffective habits of parenting be replaced by parenting philosophies and methods that work.

THREE EASY
COMMUNICATION TECHNIQUES

Everyone knows that good communication is invaluable in all relationships. So why are there so many problems with communication? People just don't know how to communicate especially with their children. For many parents "a good talking to" is their ideas of forming a positive parent – child bond. Let's first talk about what communication is.

Communication is the relating and perceiving of meaning. Its' medium is writing, vocalization, or motion. Art also communicates meaning.

Communication in a relationship is a two way street. It involves listening and hearing another's thoughts, moods, and feelings. It involves expressing your own thoughts, mood and feelings.

TECHNIQUE #1

The first technique is called **REFLECTIVE LISTEN-ING and sometimes is referred to as AFFECTIVE LISTENING and ACTIVE LISTENING.** The goal is to become a mirror to your child's feelings: the goal is to accurately reflect their affect. A formula for this is as follows:

You seem _____.

Example: You seem happy. You seem confused
(feeling or feelings)

This technique not only helps the child to see how much you care for their emotions, but opens communication from them to help them verbalize and not just act out their emotions. It also forces you as the parent to be more aware of your child's emotions.

TECHNIQUE #2

The second technique has two names. It is referred to as "I Messages" or "I Statements." With this technique, it is your opportunity to let your child, or whomever your speaking with, know how you feel as a result of their behavior and let them know what you need them to do. For example, your son our daughter misses their curfew by two hours. You could say:

"When you are late, and don't call, I worry that something happened to you. What I need from you is that you are on time and call if you absolutely can not be home on time."

Here you also see a formula:
When you _____
(1) behavior
I am _____ because _____ .
Feeling (s)   **Short Explanation of What They Did**

What I need from you is _____ .

When used properly and in conjunction with ACTIVE LISTENING your child has little to argue about. First, you are not placing blame on them as a person, only their behavior. You are maintaining respect as well as letting them know how you feel and giving them an action plan for the future.

TECHNIQUE # 3

This technique I call "Checks and Balances." I call it this because you are constantly checking with the other person if they heard you and understood and also giving them the same opportunity to keep the conversation balanced by listening to them. Here's how it works:

Child: I want to eat dinner at my friend's tonight.

Parent: What I hear you saying is that you want to eat dinner at a friend's tonight.

Child: Yes that's right.

Parent: What time is dinner and when will you be back?

Child: You are asking when will I be leaving to go to my friends.

Parent: No, I am asking when dinner is and what time you will be home.

Child: You want to know when dinner is and what time I will be home.

Parent: Exactly

Child: Dinner is at 6 and I will be home at 10.

Parent: So you will be having dinner at 6 and you will be home no later than 10 pm.

Child: Yes.

Parent: ok, have a nice time.

This too has a formula. Person A speaks and is allowed to speak <u>uninterrupted</u>. They should try to keep it short and to the point. When they have finished, they should say "I am finished" or "I am done." Person B then repeats back to person A what they heard them say. If unsatisfied, person B restates their desire or idea until person A seems to understand. Now we switch. Person B speaks or responds and says they are finished. Person A repeats back to Person B what they heard them say....

This process takes a long time to get used to and it makes conversations much longer. But, when everyone is clear, we do not have to revisit a subject. Often the simplest requests are misunderstood. For example, imagine a big family dinner. You ask the person at the end of the table to pass you the salt. Inevitably, you get the salt! However, more times than not it comes with the peppershaker too! You did not ask for nor did you want the pepper; yet someone misinterpreted what you wanted and sent both shakers down to you! If such a simple request can be messed up, imagine complex issues with massive amounts of emotion involved!

To best learn this technique, it is helpful to write it down and to have a token (foam ball for example), which is held by the person who has the "floor." It is passed to the other person once it is their turn.

COGNITIVE
BEHAVIORAL METHODS

Now, I would like to put together the information you learned on behavior modification and communication.

Method #1

This method takes a lot of patience. In fact, behavior may get worse prior to improving! But, if you stick it out, and do what this manual is saying, you will see improvement! Believe it or not you need to **completely ignore** *negative behaviors.* The child does not exist when they are misbehaving! The only exceptions to this rule is if any of the following is a result of the behavior: **1)** The child is going to hurt themselves **2)** The child is going to hurt someone else **3)** The child is going to break or harm someone else's property (They can break their own property). At this point, you intercede with the most minimal intervention that will stop the behavior. This is a good opportunity to use the communication techniques.

Now that you are ignoring all the negatives except for the 3 exceptions noted above, you will **pour** on the positive feedbacks for everything positive you see them do. After a while you will learn to interject positives such as: you have behaved very well over the last ½ hour! Thank you for playing so nicely. It was fantastic that you vacuumed without being asked!

First, I want you as the parent to get used to saying wonderful things to your child for every little thing: "I like the way you walked to the door"; and "You got dressed very quickly, thank you" and "You are being very nice to your brother." Let's look at this last one. When a child hits a sibling they are often punished right away; what happens when they are not harming their sibling but are playing nicely with them? Many times this + behavior is overlooked, or not given the same level of attention as when they hit their brother or sister.

This exercise must be done for 21 consecutive days without any breaks, stoppage etc. Keep a log of progress and see if you have seen any changes. If you see even a slight positive change in your child's behavior, then continue this method until they move out!

Though there is a lot of "bookkeeping" don't stop; the paperwork is worth your child's positive behavior!

One of the side effects from this technique is that we see our children mimicking **our new** behaviors. They begin saying positive things habitually!

METHOD #2

This method can be used in conjunction with the method #1.Many children, and adults need a visual component. You will need 3 items, a mechanical timer such as an egg timer, a clear plastic container at least ½ quart in size, and a bag of jellybeans or other fun item that can be used as a token.

For children under second grade it is best to divide the day into 2 –3 sections and run this technique that many times.

You must determine how many minutes your child can behave well without intervention. For example, you may determine that 10 minutes is how long he or she can go without misbehaving. Whatever it is cut it in half! The idea is to make it **extremely easy for a child to succeed!**

In this example it is 5 minutes! We know that there are 12 five-minute periods in an hour and in 4 hours there are 48. In 8 hours there are 96 and in 12 hours there are 144. You must decide based on your child's age or attention span, how long of an interval you will use for him/her. For our example we will use 4 hours.

We set the timer for five minutes. Each time it rings, the child **and you** put a jellybean, or another *token of success*, into the container. When the timer rings you need to decide if your child has been behaving. If yes, you put the bean in together and give a verbal and if possible a physical affirmation (hug, kiss) and let them know how wonderful they have behaved! If their behavior has been challenging, you reset the timer, tell them they did not do so well and that **you know they will do better this time** and that if they do you will give them two (2) beans! At the end of the 4-hour interval, if your child has been good they should have 48 jellybeans! But, what if they only have thirty? Well, you will require only ½ the jellybeans or 24 to succeed! We want them to have to go tremendously out of their way not to succeed. We want them to understand that we want them to succeed. As a reward they get to eat a few beans. They also get a reward: Taking a walk with you, reading a story, watching an appropriate movie…

Now, as your child gets use to the program, you can increase the minutes on the timer by 1 –2 minutes until you are up to 15 minutes! Now at 15 minutes, the 4 hours yields 12 jellybeans! So remember to also tell them that they have been doing so well that you are going to give them 3 beans each time the bell rings! They will think this is a reward and it will reinforce positive behavior! Once you have arrived at 30 minutes you can begin increasing the amount of beans needed to get a reward to ¾. In other words, they will need 75% of the total possible *tokens of success* to get a reward instead of 50%. So in the above exercise if they get 6 beans every 30 minutes they could get a total of 48 in four hours.

Instead of requiring at least 24 beans, you require 36. Now you have successfully modified your child's behavior from 5 minutes to 30 minutes and he needs to behave well 75% of the time instead of a minimum of 50%! Never, should you insist on a perfect score! Why? Because no one is perfect!! However, you could sweeten the pie for a perfect score by offering a great reward! Very importantly never ever take away a reward once it is earned!

This technique is mobile and can be taken to the store or to visit relatives.

This exercise must be done for 21 consecutive days without any breaks, stoppage etc. Keep a log of progress and see if you have seen any changes. If you see even a slight positive change in your child's behavior, then continue this method!

METHOD # 3

This method is used for older kids or for kids who see the above methods as childish or are not responding. This method is called **NO PRIVILEGE!** At first glance, the methods described above seem more positive than method # 3. However this method instills the notion of _responsibility_! When things get difficult, or when your child responds positively to this method, use the techniques for communication above, to strengthen this method. This is a great method for older children.

First make a list of all the privileges your child has. Actually it is easier to write what is required for a child and the rest are privileges. For example the following are privileges: Playing sports, using the telephone, eating desert, playing with friends, watching TV or movies, listening to music, having your laundry done by someone else, etc.

As parents, one of the techniques we have used is taking away privileges. When we do this we become the immediate _bad guy_ and we are setup for the fall. Let's say we turn this around and your children have no privileges. They can either earn them, like a paycheck is earned, or they go without them.

How this works is that on Sunday your child has no privileges and must earn them Sunday for Monday. If they earn them, by meeting 75% - 80% of expectations, they **must** get them. You cannot withhold Monday's earned privileges (unless your child does something horrendous!). If you worked Sunday, and failed to go to work on Monday, you would still expect to be paid for Sunday!

Now, if your child fails to earn his or her privileges, you will be as disappointed as they and let them know that you would be happy to give them their privileges if they had earned them! Tell them that you have faith they will earn them for tomorrow!

Both you and your child must have concrete measurable behavioral expectations and I recommend they be written down. They should always be worded in a positive manner. For example, instead of "Joseph will not leave his plate for someone else to clean" you would write "Joseph will clear his plate and put it in the dishwasher immediately after eating." *Always include the following "Joseph will treat other's with respect." This helps you show him that this value trait must always be part of his behavioral repertoire.

This exercise must be done for 21 consecutive days without any breaks, stoppage etc. Keep a log of progress and see if you have seen any changes. If you see even a slight positive change in your child's behavior, then continue this method until they move out!

The rest is up to you. You need to follow this booklet exactly. It is very formulated and some of the exercises will be uncomfortable. It is important to take a look at yourself and how you relate to others, to your spouse, to your friends and to your children. You are the most important role model that your children have. None of these techniques will work very well unless you have "your own house in order." If marital problems exist, get counseling from a good marital or family counselor. Remember the following and perhaps it will help you to continue using these methods and techniques:

1. If you keep on doing what you've always done, you will always get what you always got!

2. The definition of insanity: Doing the same thing over and over again expecting different results!

3. Do what you expect your children to do: Be an example!

4. Ask Yourself "Who's the Role Model?"

5. Can you envision how you would like things to be?

6. Are you doing things like a scientist or are you taking short cuts?

7. Need additional help; keep reading....

SHOW RESPECT AT ALL TIMES

TALK TO ADULTS WITH RESPECT

ASK FIRST

USE COMMUNICATION TECHNIQUES

POSITIVE BEGETS POSITIVE!

ONE PERSON SPEAKS AT A TIME

YOU SEEM _____
              FEELING(S)

I FEEL _____
         FEELING(S)

WHEN YOU _____
            (1)BEHAVIOR

BECAUSE _____.

I NEED YOU TO _____

List of Feelings

Happy	Keen	Ashamed	Fuming
Festive	Earnest	Useless	Stubborn
Contented	Intent	Worthless	Belligerent
Relaxed	Zealous	Ill at ease	Confused
Calm	Ardent	Weepy	Awkward
Complacent	Avid	Vacant	Bewildered
Satisfied	Anxious	Hurt	Fearless
Serene	Enthusiastic	Injured	Encouraged
Comfortable	Proud	Isolated	Courageous
Peaceful	Excited	Offended	Confident
Joyous	Desirous	Distressed	Secure
Ecstatic	Sad	Pained	Independent
Enthusiastic	Sorrowful	Suffering	Reassured
Inspired	Unhappy	Afflicted	Bold
Glad	Depressed	Worried	Brave
Pleased	Melancholy	Crushed	Daring
Grateful	Gloomy	Heartbroken	Heroic
Cheerful	Somber	Cold	Hardy
Excited	Dismal	Upset	Determined
Cheery	heavy-hearted	Lonely	Loyal
Lighthearted	Quiet	Despair	Proud
Buoyant	Mournful	tortured	Impulsive
Carefree	Dreadful	Pathetic	Interested
Surprised	Dreary	Angry	Concerned
Optimistic	Flat	Compassion	Fascinated
Spirited	Blah	Resentful	Engrossed
Vivacious	Dull	Irritated	Intrigued
Brisk	In the dumps	Enraged	Absorbed
Sparkling	Sullen	Furious	Excited
Merry	Moody	Annoyed	Curious
Generous	Sulky	Inflamed	Inquisitive
Hilarious	Out of Sorts	Provoked	Creative
Exhilarated	Low	Sullen	Sincere
Jolly	Discontented	Indignant	Doubtful
Playful	Discouraged	Irate	Unbelieving
Elated	Disappointed	Wrathful	Skeptical
Jubilant	Concerned	Cross	Distrustful
Thrilled	Sympathetic	Sulky	Suspicious
Restful	Resolve	bitter	Dubious
Silly	choked up	Frustrated	Uncertain
Giddy	Embarrassed	Grumpy	Questioning
Eager	Shameful	Boiling	Evasive

Wavering	Nauseated	Envious	Hysterical
Hesitant	Sluggish	Jealous	Alarmed
Perplexed	Weary	Preoccupied	Cautious
Indecisive	Repulsed	Cruel	Shocked
Hopeless	Tired	Distant	Horrified
Powerless	Alive	Bored	Insecure
Helpless	Firm	Hypocritical	Impatient
Defeated	Hard	Phony	Nervous
Pessimistic	Light	Two-faced	Dependent
Confused	Affectionate	Cooperative	Anxious
Physical	Soft	Burdened	Pressured
Taut	Close	Played out	Worried
Uptight	Loving	Hopeful	Suspicious
Immobilized	Sexy	Afraid	Hesitant
Paralyzed	Tender	Fearful	Awed
Tense	Seductive	Frightened	Dismayed
Stretched	Warm	timid	Scared
Hollow	Open	Wishy-washy	Cowardly
Empty	Appealing	Shaky	Threatened
Frisky	Aggressive	Apprehensive	Appalled
Strong	Passionate	Fidgety	Petrified
Weak	Humble	Terrified	Gutless
Sweaty	Torn	Panicky	Edgy
Breathless	Mixed-up	Tragic	

Feelings  **Can Be**

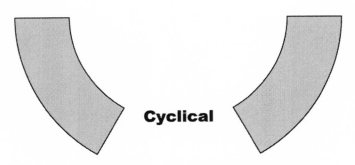 **Cyclical**

Do You Notice Any Patterns?

NOTES:

CONCLUSION AND SPECIAL OFFER

This Manual was made as a quick reference to give direction and hope to parents with difficult parenting challenges. It is not meant to replace needed counseling and family therapy. In addition, it was not written to include every possible parenting scenario.

With the purchase of this book, you receive a free 20 minute telephone consultation. Focus will be on your parenting questions and an opportunity to tweak your parenting interventions to better fit your situation. Continued consultations are available for a minimal fee. To contact Mr. Raskind email him at michaelraskind@gmail.com and leave a telephone number; best times to call and a 1 -2 paragraph explanation of your situation and any questions you may have.

Notes for Conference

21534954R00038

Made in the USA
Middletown, DE
13 December 2018